MadeEasy Series

Words of Knowledge

MadeEasy

Scott Thompson

Copyright

Endorsement

"There are few men I have seen that are as anointed and gifted to release people into the things of the supernatural as my friend Scott Thompson. Year after year, we have had the privilege of having Scott teach and train people at our Jesus Culture conferences with profound results and impact. He has a grace to equip not only people that have never experienced healing or walking in the power of

God but also to help people continue to go deeper in the things of the supernatural. It is critical the Body of Christ walk in the power of God and the gifts of the Spirit if we are to see cities saved and nations transformed. Scott makes the supernatural accessible and ignites courage and faith in people to believe God for greater things."

Banning Liebscher

Director of Jesus Culture

Contents

For My Family

I would love to take this chance to recognize my wonderful family who support the call of God on my life and constantly teach me to see God in new ways.

Thank you to my amazing wife Lacey "The Hotness" who has supported me unlike any other person in my life. You are the love of my life and the one person who has shown me what true love really looks like in a relationship. I am honored to spend the rest of my life with such an honest, genuine and faithful woman. You inspire me and cause me to be a better person.

Orren the worshipper, Judah the preacher and Ava my artist; you kids make this Dad so happy. I thank God that I get to be your Dad. You each, in your own way, have shown me aspects of God that have changed my life. Thank you for loving me and continuing to show me God through your life. You are going the turn this world upside down! Daddy loves you.

Thanks

I would like to thank everyone who helped make this manual possible. Sheryl "Nana" Roan for being a source of love and for editing this manual, David Edwards for layout, cover, all his help and for being such a supportive friend, Banning Liebscher for his endorsement and for constantly seeing more in me than I see in myself.

I would also like to thank the Moms and Dads in my life: My mom Gail Gibbons, my dad Billy Thompson, Sheryl & Tom Roan, Bill Tamagni, Grandma & Grandpa Thompson, Steve & Becky Helton, Banning Liebscher, Steve & Lindy Hale, Ron & Carolyn Book, Leif & Jennifer Hetland. You have all been a constant encouragement and have all helped me become the man I am today. Words cannot express how thankful I am.

Intro

      This manual is the first in a series of manuals written to help you understand God more and bring you into a deeper relationship with Him. It focuses on helping you to understand the gift of Words of Knowledge, as well as causing you to begin to operate easily in them. I have the honor of traveling the world, both with Jesus Culture and my own personal ministry, to train people to walk in the power of

God. I have equipped tens of thousands of people and sent them out on the streets over the last 10 years. Some of the ones sent out have never even prayed for anyone before. Amazingly, they return with some of the craziest testimonies of God's love and power.

One summer, I trained a group of young people at a camp in Georgia and sent them out to activate what they had learned. Two young Catholic girls were at the camp that year that didn't really believe God would speak to them or use them. I asked them to just humor me and give it a try. When I requested everyone to write a list of things God was showing them, they said, "Fine, we'll just make something up." So, I told them, "Thank you." Finally, they wrote down, "Man in wheelchair." Next, I released the group to go and find the things on the list God had showed them. As they went, one of the girls suggested that they go shopping at the thrift store. When they got there, they were happy to find that they were the only customers in the store.

As they began looking at clothes, they heard the door ding as another customer arrived. When they turned around, a man was being pushed into the store by his wife in a wheelchair. They freaked out because I told them if they saw what they wrote on their list they would have to pray for the person. They didn't believe anything was going to happen, but they agreed that they would.

As they walked up to the man they told him how they were supposed to look for a person in a wheelchair and when they found him they were suppose to pray for him. They had heard me tell a few testimonies of people getting out of wheelchairs earlier at the camp, so they went for it. Although they had never prayed for anyone before, they prayed a brief prayer and then asked the man to try to stand up, just like they had heard in the testimonies.

They didn't know any different! They didn't really give the man much choice. They just grabbed him by the hands and started helping him out of his wheelchair. He stood up and his wife started crying heavily. The man had a wild look on his face and he told the two girls that he hadn't stood in over a decade. They were so excited they asked him to try to walk. He took his first steps slowly as his wife stood by sobbing. The more he walked the more natural it got for him. The girls were freaking out, the wife was crying big alligator tears, and the man was rejoicing loudly. The wife told the girls that for a decade she had helped him do everything, all day, every day. She had bathed him, moved him from his chair to bed, helped him in the bathroom, helped feed him, and everything else. Now, she was watching this same man walk around the thrift store. The experience ended with the man walking his own wheelchair out to their van on his own. The wife was still crying and smiling as they drove away. The girls came back screaming in excitement and crying as they told me the crazy story. How cool is that? God used two Catholic girls, who humored me, to go out on outreach and end up seeing a man that had a severed spinal cord receive a miracle.

I have witnessed young people get saved in a service, then sit through a brief training, before being sent out on the streets to see the power of God displayed. It's wild to see freshly saved young Christians, without any history of ministry experience or training, start their Christian life by seeing God move powerfully when they pray. I know without a doubt that the difference between those who see miracles and those who do not is the simple fact that the ones stepping out are the ones seeing the miracles. The people that are listening are the people that are hearing God. In this manual, I am trying to keep the instruction as simple as possible. Walking in power does not have to be hard. It's not so much about WHAT you know as it is about WHO you know. It's not about who you are; it's about whose you are. My prayer is that this "Made Easy" manual would help bring you into a deeper relationship with God that makes you sensitive to him and the way he communicates to you.

Words of

<u>Knowledge</u>

Loving Father

The exciting thing about the Christian life is that we, unlike other "religions," have a living and active God who desires a relationship with us. That's something to be excited about! We aren't ruled by a dictator, but we are invited into a loving relationship with a personal, caring, and intimate Father. One of the greatest honors we have is being called to co-labor with Him in the harvest of souls. We have a good Dad and we get to share His goodness with the people around us. He doesn't just send us out into the "world" helpless and on our own. He invites us to go out with Him. He fills us with His presence and gives us gifts to bear fruit.

Spiritual Gifts

In 1 Corinthians 12 the spiritual gifts are listed. It is important to see that it is very clear in Corinthians that the gifts operate through the Holy Spirit. There are a variety of gifts, but the same Spirit. It is the Holy Spirit that empowers the gifts to be active in us. To EACH is given the manifestation of the Spirit for the common good.

The list of gifts in Corinthians is as follows:

"For to one is given through the Spirit the utterance of wisdom, and to another the utterance of knowledge according to the same Spirit, to another Faith by the same Spirit, to another gifts of healing by the same Spirit, to another working of miracles, to another prophecy, to another the ability to distinguish between spirits, to another various kinds of tongues, to another the interpretation of tongues. All these are empowered by one and the same Spirit, who apportions to each one individually as he wills."

1 Corinthians 12:8-11 ESV

Each gift is given to man to "manifest" or display the nature of God. It is important to know that "God is love." This keeps love the focus while desiring and operating in spiritual gifts. Knowing and walking in love, is knowing your Father's love for you, developing a relationship with Him, and walking in His will.

Pursue Love

1 Corinthians 14 puts it in a context that we should pay close attention to. It is a healthy order that should be our motivation in pursuing spiritual gifts.

"Pursue love, and earnestly desire the spiritual gifts, especially that you may prophesy. For one who speaks in a tongue speaks not to men but to God; for no one understands him, but he utters mysteries in the Spirit. On the other hand, the one who prophesies speaks to people for their upbuilding and encouragement and consolation. The one who speaks in a tongue builds up himself, but the one who prophesies builds up the church. Now I want you all to speak in tongues, but even more to prophesy. The one who prophesies is greater than the one who speaks in

tongues, unless someone interprets, so
that the church may be built up."

1 Corinthians 14:1-5 ESV

It is imperative that we pursue love
because the Bible says God IS love. Love is not
just something that He participates in, but He
actually IS love. Love is not an emotion or
activity that God chooses. Love does not exist
outside of God. He is love and when we pursue
God we are pursuing love.

Greater Gifts

There are many spiritual gifts, but the
greatest gifts in this passage from Corinthians
are the ones that have impact on the people
around us. The Gift of Prophecy in this section
is being specifically compared to the Gift of
Speaking in Tongues, but it paints a great
picture to look at all the other gifts through. A

gift that is for self-development is great; although, an even greater gift is one that encourages the people around us. Therefore, a Word of Knowledge can be used as a greater gift because it can build up those around us. God gives knowledge to us about another, revealing to that person that God knows them. In my experience with Words of Knowledge, I have seen a lot of people healed. However, maybe the greatest thing I have seen is people experiencing through a Word of Knowledge that God really knows and cares for them. It shows that His spotlight is shining down on them!

A Word of Knowledge is knowledge from God that can be for your own good or for the good of the people around you. It gives you knowledge about things Holy Spirit is highlighting to you. These are things you would not know without the Spirit of God illuminating them to you.

Master Communicator

The still small voice of God can be heard in so many different ways. Here are a few of the ways God speaks: audibly, physical feeling, divine imaginations, open visions, wisdom, knowledge, dreams, emotions, other people, the Word, music, art, and visual prompts. This list is not all-inclusive, so allow it to open up your expectation for God to speak to you in more ways than English. In the next section, I will walk you through the list and give description for each item, but first I want to share a testimony with you of how God reached me on a firefighting bus, by speaking to me creatively.

Testimony

I had a substantial encounter with God that led to my salvation. I was a suicidal young man at the time. I was selling and using a lot of different drugs and had given up on life.

I had a job doing Wildland Firefighting and I had reached the end of myself while on a fire that I was fighting. My whole crew had gotten an extremely bad case of poison oak. Then, adding insult to injury, we all caught the flu. It was a horrible experience!

Our crew leader decided that it was time to leave the fire after about 18 days of hard 20 hour work days. We were a sight to see. We hadn't showered in a long time, working 20 hour days, covered in poison oak, and sick with the flu. The smell coming from our crew was even worse. We were camping on the top of a large mountain and the only way down was for our crew to drive down the mountain in a bus on a narrow Jeep/ATV trail. Everyone was scared that our bus was going to end up rolling down the side of the mountain and we were all going to die. I, on the other hand, was actually thinking it would be a good time to be done with my life.

I was sitting on the bus with my headphones in, listening to a song by a band named Slipknot. The song made me start contemplating life and I decided to ask God a question. I asked Him, "God, where the hell have you been?" Right then I looked out the window to see a small creek running along side our bus. On the edge of the creek were two sets of animal tracks. I noticed that one of the sets of tracks stopped while the other set continued on. The scene reminded me of a poem I had read as a kid called *Footprints*.

The poem talks about a guy that is walking down the beach with God. He looks back over his life and sees that at the hardest times in his life there were only one set of footprints. He asked God why He left him at the hardest times in his life. God answered back, "I didn't leave you. When there was only one set of footprints, I was carrying you."

When that poem came to my mind, I immediately started to cry. This was unexpected because I hadn't cried in at least a few years. My emotions had become numb over time. It was such a surprise to me so I quickly put my sunglasses on. I didn't want any one else on the fire crew to see I was crying. That's when it all began. I started to experience memories of the significant events in my life. I was not just remembering them in my mind, I was having the experiences all over again. They were more than just open visions. I was still on the fire bus, but I was also back at the time it happened. They were as real as the first time. It was one experience after another. In each one, God was showing me that He was with me. Some of the experiences were good and some were traumatic, but God was there for all of them. In the good, he was celebrating with me, and in the bad, he was hurting with me. It was the most intense experience of my life. His love in those experiences answered my question and caused me to stop running from him. I had six hours of an extreme encounter with the God of the universe and He didn't even have to use words to communicate with me. He is so creative that He is not confined to any language or communication medium. The way He chose to speak to me included a Slipknot song, nature, the fact that I was stuck on a bus for six hours, my emotions, my frustration, a question, my imagination, my senses, my past experiences, and His love. All of which communicated a profound message of love to me. That is why we need to learn to look and listen for God in creative ways.

Communication

Now, let's go over a list of ways God speaks to us. This list is not an "end all," but it should get you out of the box of just listening for communication in English. Your body, mind, and spirit can become a finely tuned instrument for intimate communication with God. Please invite God to take you on a journey of understanding Him and the different ways he communicates.

Audibly

The audible voice is simply God speaking to you out loud. God spoke audibly many times in the Bible. (Exodus 3:14 - God speaks to Moses; Joshua 1:1 - God appoints Joshua leader after the death of Moses; Judges 6:18 - Gideon asks the Lord to wait for Him and the Lord replies; 1 Samuel 3:11 - The Lord speaks to Samuel; and the list goes on.) Please take the time to read a few of these Biblical examples of God speaking out loud to his people.

Physical Sensations

God can speak to us through physical touch. I have experienced the presence of God in many ways, but one of the most amazing ways God speaks to us is through letting us experience His love and touch physically. I have experienced His touch that feels like sudden warmth in my body, tingles, extreme rushes of peace, and in words of knowledge where He lets me feel where others are experiencing physical pain in their bodies. I have also felt the hand of God physically resting on my shoulder in one experience. It was as real as a Dad placing his hand on my shoulder. This happened on my first time back to church and really sealed my salvation experience for me.

Divine Imagination

The divine imagination is simply God using your imagination creatively to speak to you. Everyone has the movie screen in our minds where we imagine or recount experiences. If I were to describe to you a large grassy field with small light blue flowers scattered throughout and a large oak tree right in the middle of it, then you would begin to put the picture together visually in your imagination. God can give you a picture in your imagination as a form of communication. This simply happens by you inviting God to speak to you and then opening your mind to listen even in your imagination. This is one of the main ways God speaks to me with Words of Knowledge. At first, I thought I was making it up, but then I realized that I was imagining things that I wouldn't naturally think of. Over time, I have learned to know the difference between my imagination and my divinely inspired imagination.

Open Visions

I experience open visions often. An open vision is different than divine imagination. While divine imagination takes place in your mind, an open vision is a vision you see with your physical eyes. This often freaks people out, but I have gotten used to it. I have found the less I try to make it happen, the more it happens. The more time you spend with God the more you realize that the spiritual world is so much more real than what you experience physically. People who open themselves up to experience the creative communication of God are the ones that will experience it. Don't get discouraged if this doesn't happen right away for you. I encourage you to start where you are and be excited at the glimpses of God that you are experiencing now. If you can be excited and thankful in your present, then you are setting yourself up to experience more.

Wisdom

The Bible actually talks about a gift called Words of Wisdom. It is a gift of receiving wisdom from God. It says in the Bible that the spiritual Gift of Word of Wisdom is for the common good. It is not only to help with your circumstances, but also for you to give divinely inspired wisdom to others (1 Corinthians 12). Words of Wisdom can be perceived, or it can be a wisdom that just suddenly comes to you. It can be a gut feeling, or it can come through the audible voice of God or another person.

Knowledge

The gift of Words of Knowledge is listed with the rest of the gifts in 1 Corinthians 12. A Word of Knowledge is God highlighting information about the past or present. It is information you didn't have before He showed you. It is knowledge given about a person, place, thing, or circumstance. Sometimes God will highlight an injury in someone's body because He wants to heal them. Other times, He will show you a past event to let the person see that He knows and cares for them. It shows them that He has been there in their life.

Dreams

It's so fun to realize that your dreams are not just affected by scary movies and fear, but when we say YES to God, we are saying YES to Him in every area of our lives. God can and does speak to us through our dreams! Listen to your dreams. Keep a notepad next to your bed and if you have a problem remembering your dreams, ask God to wake you up in the night so you can write them down. God will be faithful to wake you up. I've had times where I woke up just barely enough to scribble some words down on a piece of paper, but it was sufficient to spark the memory of the dream in the morning, when I became fully awake. Some of the most profound events in my Christian walk have been accompanied by dreams given to me by God. And, as I leaned into Him for an interpretation of what the dream meant, it came. Sometimes God will give you dreams about another person that could be life transforming when shared with them.

Emotions

So many people are "feelers," but they just don't know it. A feeler is someone who feels the spiritual atmosphere or things others are going through emotionally, mentally, and physically. Have you ever walked into a room with other people in it and suddenly felt depressed or angry? You didn't feel that way before you walked in the room and you had no reason to feel that way now. Many times, you are picking up on what is in the room. You could be picking up on the fact that someone is having a hard time. Without understanding that God could speak to you about it, you could just end up questioning yourself. Once we begin to understand that God is a creative communicator, we can then be used to change atmospheres and encourage people in their time of need.

Other People

God can speak through other people. I have had God speak to me through a conversation with a homeless man, children, friends, pastors, and through other believers. Sometimes God hides the words we need in the people who will be in our lives that day. Sometimes people will be speaking the word of the Lord to you without even realizing it.

The Word

The Bible is the infallible Word of God. It is amazing that text and stories written so long ago, in such a different time in history, can still be so relevant today. God can speak through the Word for every need or question we have. It's important that we are daily running our lives through the Holy Spirit inspired Word of God.

Music

As you read earlier in my testimony, God used a Slipknot song to trigger an encounter that saved my life. If that's not being a creative communicator, then I don't know what is! God can use songs on the radio or a song in your head to speak a message to you.

Nature

Also, in my testimony, God used the creek with animal tracks next to it to remind me of a poem I read as a child. It was an example of how God uses nature to speak to us. The sun reminds us of His faithfulness when it rises, without question, every single morning. Likewise, rainbows are a sign of His promises.

The earth displays His beauty in mountains, rivers, flowers and waterfalls. When we are fully aware of God, then we will see Him displayed in nature. We will also understand that He is communicating to us through nature.

Visual Prompts

God can use signs, advertisements, landmarks buildings and other visual prompts to speak to us and guide us through our day. I could tell hours of testimonies of ways God has used visual prompts to help me find the person He wants me to pray for. It's amazing to let God lay out a course that leads you to a stranger you have never met by showing you visual prompts in advance. It can be so exciting when you set out to find the person He is highlighting and you start to see the things He has shown you along the way.

Conclusion

God has the ability to speak any way He wants. This list is just a beginning to get you thinking and looking for God outside of just using words. I want to challenge you to start to expect and look for God in your daily life. I am convinced that He is always talking to us; we just may not be always listening. God is interested in being in an intimate relationship with you. He is not only interested in knowing you fully, but also being fully known by you. Let's dive deeply together into a relationship with God and broaden the ways we hear him in our lives.

The next sections contain activations for you to use to begin to exercise your spiritual gifts.

Activation 1

For our first activation, I want you to take the next four days to heighten your awareness of God and the different ways He is speaking to you. Look for Him in your day. Listen to your dreams and keep this manual by your bedside with a pen ready to write them down. Keep a journal of the different ways God is speaking to you. No matter how small the interaction is with God, I want you to write it down. At the end of each day, review the ways he has spoken to you and begin to thank Him for them. If we can be thankful in the small encounters, our thankfulness will attract more. Remember to be open to see God in creative ways that you may not have looked for before. Just like He is not limited in the way He speaks to you, He is also not limited in where He speaks to you. He can speak to you in your alone time, but He can also speak to you in your car or at work. He can speak to you when you set aside time and when you are busy. The goal is to be available to hear God's voice at anytime.

Prayer

"Father, I want to be more aware of you. I want to be more sensitive to you and the ways you communicate with me. God open my eyes, ears, and senses to hear and see you in new ways. Holy Spirit guide me into new depths in our relationship. Be with me as I explore the different ways you speak. Amen!"

Notes: Day 1

Notes: Day 2

Notes: Day 3

Notes: Day 4

Activation 2

For this activation we are going to step into Words of Knowledge. I want you to start each day by getting alone with God and asking Him for a list of things that He wants you to look for during the day. I want you to open yourself up to get this list in different ways. Be ready to feel, imagine, sense, know, see, or whatever other form of communication God may use. Write down everything you get, even if you think that you are making it up. (It's funny how much we think we are just making up, but when given a chance you will see that most of it is usually God.)

After writing it down, take the list with you and keep an eye open for the things He has shown you. It could be someone's clothing, a person's name, a building, or a song on the radio. Each day, try to get more specific words. Take the next four days to do this. Make sure to journal your experiences. At the end of each day, go over your journal and begin to thank God for the things that were highlighted to you. Don't be discouraged if your list doesn't work. Just do it again the next day. Sometimes we have to dedicate time to gaining sensitivity with God. I promise He is speaking to you. Don't move off this exercise until you feel like it has worked well for you and you are comfortable.

Prayer

"Father, I thank you that you are speaking to me! I thank you for your love and the fact that you are so patient. God, speak to me with Words of Knowledge and help me to be sensitive to you. I want to know you more and hear you clearly. I want to be an instrument of love to the people around me. God, open me up to your world. I want to see through your eyes. Thank you father for this journey you are taking with me. Amen!"

Notes: Day 1

Notes: Day 2

Notes: Day 3

Notes: Day 4

Activation 3

Let's have some fun! This is where we start to go public with our Words of Knowledge. In this activation, I want you to get a little more specific with your words. I want you to get words for a person. I want you to ask God again for a list, just like we did in Activation 2. Start at the beginning of your day. The difference this time is going to be that you are asking Him for a list of words for a person you know. You are not just asking for a list of things He wants to show you to confirm that he is speaking. You are asking for a list to minister to someone else. Rather than starting with a stranger, we will go easy on this activation and ask God to show you someone you know. Ask God who to minister to and what He wants to tell you for that person.

You are not getting prophetic words. Prophetic words are about the future. Words of Knowledge are past and present. The idea of this activation is to use your Words of Knowledge to begin to show others that God knows them and cares for them. This should be encouraging to whomever He gives you to minister to.

I want you to try to stay away from highlighting any past or present sin, and finding failure in someone. I would like you to focus on the love of God and interact with people from that place. If He gives you a Word of physical pain or illness, I want you to ask them if the Word is true. If it is, follow up by praying for healing. This should be a safe and easy way to start since you will know the person. If you get the opportunity to pray for healing, please know that we don't have to beg God or question whether or not He wants to heal the person. If He is giving you the Word of Knowledge about it, then He is saying He wants to do something about it. He does not bring things up just to talk about them. He brings things up because He is the ultimate answer to them. Have fun encouraging others with Words from the Father!

Before you begin, here is another testimony to spark your faith for this activation.

Testimonies

At Bethel Atlanta, in our school of ministry, we have our students get in pairs and ask God for Words of Knowledge for one another. One time, God gave a student a picture of a light-blue farmhouse on a gravel road. It had a large tree out front with a tire swing hanging from a branch. Upon sharing the word, the feedback from the other student revealed that it was their family house, the one they lived in as a child. Everything about the picture was exact! They were so encouraged by this.

We have heard some of the craziest words. I would encourage you to step out no matter how weird the word sounds. Sometimes it won't make much sense to you, but it will speak profoundly to the other person.

Another night, when we were practicing Words of Knowledge, we instructed our students to pair up again and ask God what the other student's favorite toy was while growing up. One of the students felt like the Lord said the name Bernard. When the student shared the name with his partner, she immediately started crying. She was crying because earlier that week she had found her childhood Teddy Bear and was trying to remember it's name. All she could remember was that the Bear's name started with the letter "B." The name that God gave her partner was the name of her teddy bear! It profoundly spoke to the girl and showed how God knows her so well.

As you do this activation, I want to ask you not to get discouraged if you don't get all your Words right. This is a learning experience. It's just like walking and talking for the first time. It can take a while to be great at it. Give yourself grace and mercy, while celebrating the little successes.

Prayer

"Father thank you for the ways you have spoken to me so far. Thank you for bringing me to a deeper place with you. I now see that you really are speaking to me regularly. God, I want to begin to impact others with these words. Father, highlight the people in my life that you want to speak to and give me words of encouragement for them. God, let me be one who shares a Word of Knowledge to show that You know the people I minister to. God, I pray that You would receive glory from this time. Amen!"

Notes: Day 1

Notes: Day 2

Notes: Day 3

Notes: Day 4

Activation 4

Okay so, at this point you have started to pay attention to the different ways God speaks. You have gotten lists to look for in your day. You have stepped out and ministered to people you know with Words of Knowledge. Now it's the time you have been waiting for! It's time to minister to strangers. For some of you this will be very easy. Others may be a little timid to walk up to a complete stranger. You can do this! The Holy Spirit will give you courage and you will not be alone. The most powerful thing you can be is yourself. You don't have to look or act like anyone else. God wants to use you. I have seen God use someone's shyness as a powerful strength. When they shyly walked up to pray for a stranger, the stranger saw they were shy and came closer to them. God does not send you out by yourself. You need to know that all of heaven backs you as you step out. For this activation I want you to combine all three of the previous activations. Be sensitive to God. Ask Him what you are going to see in your day. This is the fun part. Instead of just seeing things on your list, use your list as confirmation that you are on the right track. In this activation your list will lead you to the people you are going to minister to.

I have had the privilege to work with Jesus Culture and send thousands of young people out onto the streets with Words of Knowledge to pray for others. I have heard some of the most amazing testimonies from the teams that have gone out. I can honestly say that some of the most profound testimonies have come from people that have never experienced anything like this before.

When I send people out for Jesus Culture, they go without ever doing the first three activations you have done in this manual. They are going out "cold turkey!" So, you have received more training in this short manual than any teams I have ever sent out. The following testimonies are examples of some those trainings.

Testimonies

Years ago at Jesus Culture in Redding, California, I took a team out to a small shopping center. I asked if everyone had gotten words and asked a few people to share their words. One of the groups shared their words and the list looked like this: American flag shirt, white pants, red shoes, an American flag hat holding a small American flag, dead oak tree, stop light and pain in the neck.

I thought this must be bunk. It was not the Fourth of July so I figured they were never going to find anyone dressed like that. Also, we were in a parking lot with pretty little landscaped trees and there were no dead oak trees in sight. So, I decided to go with this group because I thought they were going to need help, since they didn't have any words that I expected to actually see take place.

As we walked off, we ran into a man just a little ways down the sidewalk who had on the exact outfit described in the list. He looked like Uncle Sam. He was just standing there on the sidewalk. We started talking to the man and said a brief prayer for him and then felt like we were suppose to move on and continue with our list.

Next, we walked out to the stop light like the list said. As we crossed the street, we spotted a huge dead oak tree behind the gas station on the other side of the street. We all got excited because we knew we were on the right track! We walked up to the gas station and there was no one in the parking lot, so we went inside.

The only people in the gas station were the clerks. The group was scared to approach them, so I went up and asked if anyone had pain in their neck. One of the ladies asked why, and I just knew the word was for her. While I was telling her how God told us we were suppose to pray for her neck, God revealed to me that her neck hurt because she was carrying a financial burden. He was going to heal her neck to show her that His intention was to change her situation. I proceeded to tell her everything I was getting from God and she started crying. I prayed for her and her neck was immediately healed. All the stiffness and pain left completely! She was so excited. The team was excited too and we were all jumping around.

She had a massive encounter with a loving heavenly Father because we chose to look for a crazy list of things. None of the list made any sense to any of us, but God had made a master list to lead us to His little girl who He wanted to heal and encourage. It is such an honor to walk with God and see people's lives change.

Another time in Cleveland, a team of girls went out with a list of words they had received. The list was a red balloon, a black and white cow, yellow flowers, and a green shirt. They went to the mall to look for their list. After they spent about an hour at the mall with no luck at all, they got discouraged and decided to head back to the church.

On the way back, they were talking about how worthless the outreach was and they crumbled up the list and threw it on the floor of the car. As they were driving, they got stuck at a red light. They said it was the longest red light ever. The light just stayed red and it wasn't changing. One of the girls in the back seat looked over and saw a gentleman in his front yard wearing a green shirt and planting flowers. Not thinking anything of it, she looked back straight. Then something caught her eye. There was a red balloon tied to the front porch and it had a picture on it. She was trying to figure out what the picture was when the balloon slowly turned to where she could see. It was a picture of a black and white cow on the red balloon. Just then the light changed to green. She freaked out and screamed to her friends. When they looked and saw the list of items, they freaked out too. They pulled the car over and walked to the house.

As they approached the man, they weren't sure what to say. One of the girls said, "Excuse me." As the man turned around, she explained that they had gotten a list of items from God and they had been looking for them. As they handed him the list to see, one of the girls said, "You are on our list and we just wanted to tell you that Jesus loves you." As she said that, the man was reading the list. With tears in his eyes, he looked up from the list and said, "I can't believe this." He explained that the only family he had was his older brother. He said that every day his brother would call and talk to him and at the end of each call his brother would tell him that Jesus loves him. He said he never really wanted to hear that because he didn't believe in God. He told them that his brother passed away the night before and someone had given him the balloon and flowers to try to cheer him up. He felt lost and didn't know what to do so he came outside to plant the flowers. He said, "And now you are coming to me with this list to tell me that Jesus loves me."

The man was in the crisis of his life and he had an encounter with God in his time of greatest need. It all happened from a silly list that wouldn't have meant anything to anyone else. The girls stayed and ministered to the man for awhile; praying for him and hugging him while he cried. It was a beautiful time for the man and the team. His brother's words became real to him and he felt the love of God. Yay God!

Prayer

"Father, I want people to know how much you love them. God, use me to be love to this world. Continue to speak to me and let me encourage others. God, I want to step out in boldness. Holy Spirit, fill me with boldness and help me step past the fear of man. I'm listening and I'm ready God. I thank you that you are the healer. I thank you that you know every need. God, let me be one who loves your kids well. Amen!"

Notes: Day1

Notes: Day 2

Notes: Day 3

Notes: Day 4

Conclusion

First, I want to thank you for making it to the end of this manual. Hopefully, this has been a great training tool for you to step deeper into Words of Knowledge and communicating with God. My desire is that the lessons you learned in this manual would be locked in your heart to become a way of life.

The world needs to see how well our Father loves and God will use you to show them. We are living in a time when God has set the stage for the greatest movement in all of history. You have been born for a time such as this. I pray that you will be bold as a lion and continue to love people into a relationship with our Father. Remember the gift of Words of Knowledge is a ministry gift for others to experience God. It is not a way for us to receive praise. Let the world see your good works and glorify your Father in heaven.

Scott
Thompson

Scott & Lacey Thompson are Associate Leaders and School of Ministry instructors at Bethel Church in Atlanta. Scott and Lacey have three children, Orren, Judah & Ava. Scott is on the Senior Leadership Team for Jesus Culture and speaks in conferences worldwide. He is a dynamic leader who operates in the prophetic and moves in signs and wonders. There is a calling on his life to break the chains off of a generation and see them preach the authentic gospel through radical love and demonstrations of power.

Made in the USA
Lexington, KY
22 March 2015